COFFEE WITH GOD

by

RANDY RAN

THE EXPANDED EDITION

This book is dedicated to

Madalene Cecelia Thomas

Also

My mom and dad

Dina and Lou

My brother and sisters

Dana, Kenya and Mary

In June of 2007, I finally decided that I was done with the relationship I had so intimately developed with the disease of addiction. I had been courted, engaged and married to an entity that had no actual physical body, but it had a spiritual malady that had taken over my life. I had no idea that it was capable of such devastation, pain, manipulation and death, and not just actual death, but the death of my soul. I noticed the change in my heart and the things that I had once cared about, the compassion I once had for others in my life. I found the quality of my life no longer existed and that the only thing that ultimately mattered was the mind altering substances that I needed to put into my body.

At first it was a subtle introduction, watching others as they would drink beverages that I wasn't allowed to drink, and how they would change their spiritual and mental being. I watched as the consumption of these beverages became a staple at social gatherings, and they were served in special glasses, or served in colorful cans with a pop top. I noticed that many people would change their attitudes and they would laugh loudly and have lots of fun with whatever they were doing. I was just a kid at the time, but I wanted to have fun like the adults were having fun. So much that we as kids sometimes "acted" the way some of the adults were acting after a few drinks.

At an early age I heard the word many times but I had no idea "alcoholic" would someday be a word to describe the person I had become. I heard the word not so often but I

had no idea the word "addict" would
someday be used to describe what I am.

In 30 years I learned a lot of things about my
life and who I had become, I am not proud
of the things I did, but I am proud that I can
now admit that I made lots of mistakes. I
know that my parents raised me to be a
responsible and respectable child of God.
They tried to instill in me the qualities of a
compassionate, honest and trusting human
being. I took all those qualities and traits, and
used them to manipulate and become a
"soul" controlled by mind altering
substances, because my disease made me to
think that it was a way to overcome my
"identity crisis". My disease taught me, if I
wanted to be somebody, I had to act like
somebody else.

~~~RENOVATION~~~

When I first decided that I wanted to change the person I had become, I associated the process with construction. Since I was familiar with how to build things I knew that every strong structure needs to have an even stronger foundation. However my "earth suit" had already been constructed, but I needed to rebuild, I needed to "RENOVATE". Starting with my foundation, I found that my foundation would only be as strong as my faith. I developed a new and deeper relationship with God and I knew it had to be continuous, unlike in the past, only when needed.

I started out talking with God every night while I lay in my bed at the residential recovery center, the place where He guided me. I would talk with Him just as I would talk with someone in conversation. This was to be the beginning of the renovation process that I needed to fill the voids in my life. There was going be some doubts at first as to whether I could have faith and trust in God. I needed to gather some tools to get started in the rebuilding of my heart and soul.

No matter what obstacles I faced on a daily basis there was some tool that God would give me and I would somehow find a place to use it later on. This was the rebuilding of things I had learned earlier in life that may have been burned away along with the bridges from my past. I needed to understand that every problem didn't have to result in anger, every decision didn't have to result in regret, and it wasn't how I was treated, it was how I reacted that made me a better person.

This was the rebuilding of my mind, my body and my soul, and this was how I learned to understand that God will give a tool to handle any and all obstacles. As each and every day would have me facing life on life's terms, I came to the realization that everyone has days with ups and downs.

~~~REDEMPTION~~~

Once I began the renovation process of my life, I also had to keep in mind that I had done a lot of damage in the wake, during destruction of my past. I had made true friendships deteriorate and family relationships a very uncomfortable way of life. There were family gatherings that I knew I wouldn't be welcomed with open arms, but rather a reluctance to attend. So became the alienation or the isolation I had initiated myself by not wanting to be a part of, and this allowed my disease to do further destruction in my heart and soul.

I know in the process of redemption I need to become accountable for the issues I caused with family and friends, either through dishonesty or manipulation. This means that mistakes I made, I need to learn from those mistakes, so that my history does not repeat itself. I so much want to change the person that I once was, and while doing so I will find myself needing to make amends to many people.

Redeeming the life I once had, to the new way of life I have now, will be a life time journey. Redemption is a tool of motivation, not just to meet the approval of everyone, but to know I can be somebody without having to be somebody else.

~~~BALANCE~~~

I know God makes things happen, and He allows things to happen

With renovation and redemption, I have other tools that I have gathered and put into my tool box, and one of the important tools I need is balance. No matter the daily issues or obstacles I may face, maintaining my serenity and balance is also important.

On September 12, 2010 shortly after 12:00 am, my best friend, sister, and one of Gods greatest gifts, was murdered. Madalene Thomas had touched so many lives, and was an inspiration to so many, and she was loved by many and disliked by no one. It was very devastating to find out that Madalene would no longer be a part of my daily life as she had become such a big part of my life for the last 30 years. She is and always will be in my heart and I am so grateful that God allowed her in my life.

It is so unfortunate that God takes the best ones from us at those unexpected times, but what I found out was this... it is Gods will. When He allowed this tragic event to happen, He also had a bigger plan that none of us seen coming.

At the memorial event for Madalene, it was held at a park, with the accomodations we needed to present her loved ones with a gathering of "celebrity status". There were at least 1000 people in attendance, maybe more, but what God did for many of us on that day was He reunited many family and friends who had not seen or spoke in upwards of 30 years. What God did was, He took One to gather many. The blessing was Madalenes life here on earth, and the many lives she touched, she was a "life changer". The gift was just that, Madalene was a life changer. She changed my life, and through her I found out that no matter what happens in my life, God will always balance it out for me.

INTRODUCTION

I hope and pray that anyone who takes the time to read my book gets something from the messages that I have shared

My intentions are not to tell you what you need to do, but only to inspire. I don't hear Gods voice in my head, I hear Gods voice in my heart. I can't explain how or why, but it's the only way I can say it and hope you understand this is how I talk with God.

God has helped me to develop a relationship with myself, and allowed me to find out through others that life truly has meaning. He doesn't make mistakes and there are no coincidences in life. What you may find in this book maybe a tool for you, but an inspiration for someone else. We just need to know that God does have a plan and when He speaks to us and through us, it may not be right away but we will see the results in time. When we speak with God, we have His undivided attention.

There is no order in which this book is formatted. I did not put inspirations in any particular order and selections are random. It's up to you, the reader, to find a place in this book that will touch you.

The pages are not numbered, because we shouldn't count our days, but count our blessings.

Many times you may just pick up this book and open it to any page. That page may or may not pertain to you, but keep in mind it may pertain to someone else, someone that God may put in your day.

The story of **COFFEE WITH GOD**

In February of 2011, God woke me up 3 hours before my shift was to start on the first day of my new job to say thanks to him so I decided to share it with my friends on Facebook. It was inspirational to me because I was really feeling the presence of God in my life at 4:00am in the morning.

Since then I have continued to share with anyone who wants to read my "Coffee with God" and it seems there are many who have coffee with us in the morning now. This morning I would like to express my gratitude and appreciation to all of you who show love and support, not just to me but to our family that has grown from just a couple friends on that morning in February, to many thousands around the world.

I only share positive inspirations because there is already enough negativity on Facebook. Most of all I want to say, Thank You all so very much for your love and support…this was the very first "Coffee with God".

~COFFEE WITH GOD~

So I'm having coffee and breakfast with God this morning and He says to me, "Son, if you have faith and follow Me, I will take care of everything". So when it was time to go, I followed Him, then He turned and said, "Son, I shall lead you always, but you're going to have to pay for breakfast". If nobody has told you they love you today, I do and God does too!

~COFFEE WITH GOD~

This morning I want to thank God for blessing me with awesome parents! Despite all my mistakes, and all my years of addiction, they still continue to call me their son. Along with my awesome parents, I want to thank God for the family he gave me with my sister and my brother. After all I have done during my addiction, they never gave up on me, and they still continue to call me their brother.

I truly want to thank all of you who share with me every day my, "Coffee with God", you truly are my inspiration. I have heard many suggestions on ways to stay clean and sober and one of the best things I heard was to find something I'm passionate about. I am passionate about my higher power…God. I didn't find God in church, I found Him in recovery. I'm spiritual, not religious and I talk to God all the time. I don't hear voices in my head, I hear His voice in my heart and for that I found a passion to share His "voice" with my extended family.

It's not up to me to tell you how to live, I can tell you if you want a better way of life, you have to want to change your life, the things you do, and the people you hang with. Every day in life you have options, choices and decisions. When you find an option and you make a choice, only you have the final decision. It's up to you, turn your life around and make a change. Remember love is just a word until you put it between you and I, so if nobody has told you they love you today, I love you and God does too.

~COFFEE WITH GOD~

This morning I asked God about bridges. He said, "Son, life is a journey and there are many roads, some will be rough, some will be long and hard, some might be easy, call those easy street.

Some roads will have bridges and you will need to cross them to get somewhere in life. Some bridges will have a toll charge, and you might not like the toll booth operator or the way the bridge was built.

Sometimes in life you'll run into problems, situations or just an obstacle of life, son prayer is always best because I can help you to build a bridge and get over those obstacles. At some point in life you may need to cross that bridge again, you may even meet that booth operator again.

Son, throughout your life you will have to cross a few bridges, some pleasant and some not so pleasant, but burning a bridge may become a resentment, and resentments create hostages. Treat each bridge as an experience in life and those you will name "lesson learned". Some day you may be someone's bridge."

Remember, love is just a word until you put it between you and I, so if nobody has told you they love you today, I love you and God does too.

~COFFEE WITH GOD~

This morning I asked God about moving on. He said, "Son, every day will become yesterday and you must move on. Memories can be well kept secrets only if you want them to be. Keeping "skeletons" or "resentments" in your heart is not healthy, especially the things you need to let go of.

You and everyone else have a past and it will always be a part of life you can never change. Moving on means being grateful of the good, the bad, and the ugly. These become life's experiences and lessons, life will never be perfect, but appreciate what it has to give you. Moving on, means having trust and faith in Me son and loving who you are today.

Some days will be better than others, but no days have to be like they were before. Every once in a while there will be a bump, an obstacle, or maybe someone who wants you to not move on, put that on the page titled "experience". Pray on it and try to move on, put this on the page titled "lessons".

It's not how you're treated, it's how you react to it that may make you a better person. Don't make your reactions and the results go on the page titled "regrets". Remember love is just a word until you put it between you and I, so if nobody has told you they love you today, I love you and God does too.

~COFFEE WITH GOD~

This morning I asked God about life. He said, "Son, life can be like a highway, you merge in and maintain speed until you see what traffic is like. You will find in one lane some will just put life on cruise control, taking life as it comes.

Some will weave in and out, sometimes with no concern for others. Then there's the fast lane, in this lane you try to move quickly to get somewhere in life, or try to reach your goals. Sometimes you will come up behind someone and you just want them to move or get out of the way. These are the people who want to control things, because they won't let the faster traffic go by.

Your ego tells you to drive up next to them and give them the finger. God smiled and said, "Son, don't get upset and don't tailgate, this is just me telling you to slow down and take your time, I will take you where you need to be.

You don't need to run people over in life to be an achiever or become successful, it's not about who you run over, it's about who you run with".   I think I will let God drive, he knows the way, and I hope you let him drive too. Remember love is just a word until you put it between you and I, so if nobody has told you they love you today, I love you and God does too.

~COFFEE WITH GOD~

This morning I asked God about relationships. He said, "Son, relationships may come and go, and sometimes they may be just for show. Some people get stuck in a relationship and feel obligated, and things end up in a bad way. Obligation does not make a relationship, and a relationship will not complete who you are.

Some relationships won't always be compatible. It's a good idea to realize when things aren't meant to be, they just aren't meant to be. Life goes on and there are more important things in life other than becoming consumed with finding someone.

Finding a passion for something in life instead of trying to find the passion in someone, is a good start. Son, there is someone for everyone and it could be any day they walk into your life. Never knowing when this could happen, it's a good idea to treat others with respect, they might become part of a bridge you have to cross someday.

When you do find that one, take care of the blessing and treat the relationship as a gift. In some cases it may be the person you least expect, but have no expectations of anyone. Taking care of who you are should always come first and that includes the real relationship you have with Me". Remember love is just a word until you put it between you and I, so if nobody has told you they love you today, I love you and God does too.

~COFFEE WITH GOD~

This morning I asked God about passion. He said, "Son, one day a week or one day a year some people want to give thanks for the things they realize they have. The next day some just continue to go on in life as if the day before meant nothing. Sometimes in life you might want to say, "I don't want to deal with things anymore." Maybe you have found things becoming too rough or situations just coming at you from all sides.

Son, there will always be obstacles in life and you overcome them by prayer, along with prayer you must have passion. This feeling starts from inside, the love you have in your heart and the spirit in your soul.

Inside each and every person there is a yearning with a passion for life, you just have to let it out. Making someone smile or laugh is one thing, the love and passion you have for yourself and others is everything. Be proud of who you are and what you have become, a person with a passion for life and a passion for others. Learning to be thankful everyday will give you a greater passion for life". Remember love is just a word until you put it between you and I, so if nobody has told you they love you today, I love you and God does too.

Just keep telling yourself TGIF=Thank God I'm Free.

~COFFEE WITH GOD~

This morning I didn't have any questions, but God knew everything in my heart and on my mind. He said, "Son, there will be some days you have no questions, there might be something going on in your life and you're just planning your next move towards another blessed day.

Family and friends are now a very important part of your life and you have learned to appreciate the finer things in life, like a place to take a shower every day, a job, gas in your truck, food in your home, your bills are being paid on time and there are no warrants with your name on them.

Son, the reason you have no questions this morning is because it's just one of those days I have allowed you to look at your life and know you have the tools to teach you how to live life on life's terms. You now have patience and understanding of others, you are accountable for your mistakes, and you have become responsible and trustable.

Son, it's one thing to be proud but it's an even greater feeling when everyone else is proud of you also". Remember love is just a word until you put it between you and I, so if nobody has told you they love you today, I love you and God does too.

~COFFEE WITH GOD~

This morning I asked God what he had planned for me today. He said, "Son, if I told you, you wouldn't have anything to look forward too. Every day there is always a different way to experience and enjoy life. Even if your day starts off not exactly the way you had planned, expect the unexpected but don't have any expectations.

You never know who you might meet today, or whose life you're going to change in a positive way. What you might say to one person, could brighten their day, or even save their life. You never know when you might have to stop during your day and say a prayer for someone. There are special things that happen with prayer and you can be part of that.

There is always the chance you could meet someone who could become your life changer. That's why you should treat the people you meet with respect, you never know when you could meet your undercover angel.

Son, I won't tell you what I have planned for you today, but I will tell you this, don't hit the snooze button on your life, you never know what I have planned for you". Remember love is just a word until you put it between you and I, so if nobody has told you they love you today, I love you and God does too.

~COFFEE WITH GOD~

This morning I asked God what's a blessing and what's a gift? He said, "Son, anything I give you is a blessing, what you choose to do with it becomes the gift. So if you choose to pay it forward, you choose the gifts of life I have allowed to make you a better person.

Blessings won't always seem so obvious, they can come in many different ways. Even when things don't seem to be in your favor, having hope, trust and faith can become a blessing in itself. It's when you realize that every morning you wake up is a blessing, smiling on the day is the gift you can share with others. Sharing is caring and often will create other blessings for you and for others.

Son, some people will go through life and think it has no meaning, until the end and then they realize it meant everything. Understanding life will always be the blessing, how you treat yourself and others becomes the gift of life".

I hope you have a great day and know this, if you are reading this, you have been blessed with another day. Remember love is just a word until you put it between you and I, so if nobody has told you they love you today, I love you and God does too.

God doesn't give me things because I deserve them. God doesn't give me things because I think I have earned them, he blesses me with things because he loves me.

~COFFEE WITH GOD~

This morning God said, "Son, there were people in your past who took you where they wanted you to be, today there are people who will tell you where you should be, follow me son and I will take you where you need to be.

Life truly is a journey, some will call it a trip, but before you start your day tie your shoelaces so you won't trip. What I mean son is that you will have enough obstacles in your life, keep life simple, and avoid those without direction.

If you have a passion for life, then share that spirit, don't be ashamed of who you were,   be proud of who you have become.   If you have a passion for something in your life, then stick with it.

Sometimes it takes what seems like a lifetime to find happiness but it takes courage to keep it.   Others can't find happiness unless the rest of the world suffers with them.   Son, pray for their strength and that they may find happiness like you".

Remember love is just a word until you put it between you and I, so if nobody has told you they love you today, I love you and God does too.

~COFFEE WITH GOD~

This morning I asked God how will I know who are my real friends? He said, "Son, many people will hang with you, many will hug you, some will even say they are your friends, but real friends walk in when the rest of the world walks out.

Sometimes people want to be your friend and they don't know how, maybe overstepping boundaries or trying to do too much. Sometimes these can be the people who are there when no one else wants to be, be patient and have understanding is how you can be a friend. Being a friend means sometimes just being there to listen, or not telling someone what to do, but take the time and teach them how to do it.

Don't look behind you to see who has your back, look beside you and find out who walks with you". I know God walks with me. Remember love is just a word until you put it between you and I, so if nobody has told you they love you today, I love you and God does too.

~COFFEE WITH GOD~

This morning I asked God about complacency. He said, "Son, sometimes in life you just feel like the world is rotating and you're not moving with it. You put expectations on yourself and others and somewhere in between you feel like you're forgetting something. You think maybe something is missing in your life and you may even become judgmental of others around you. Son, don't feel intimidated by the inner workings of others around you, people have their own agendas.

Don't be unfair to yourself and think everything is possible, being realistic is very important and just because things aren't moving at your speed, doesn't mean things can't or won't happen. When you stop trying, that's when complacency knocks on your door. Son, some things you will fail at the first time you try, don't give up, but I suggest never try sky diving". Remember love is just a word until you put it between you and I, so if nobody has told you they love you today, I love you and God does too.

~COFFEE WITH GOD~

This morning I asked God is it ok to tell someone "I love you" and they're just a friend? He said, "Son, don't be afraid to share with others the love I have shared with you. Sharing those words with others can make the difference in how they look at life.

Friends and family need to hear those words, and it can make a difference in anyone's day, even if they are just a friend. Some people may not be comfortable with those words, but be patient and understanding. Many will go through life and never have a relationship with the words, I love you. Keep them in your prayers and remember this, handshakes are for business deals, hugs are for saving lives.

Imagine the power of telling someone I love you because the greatest distance between two people can disappear when you say, "I love you". Remember love is just a word until you put it between you and I, so if nobody has told you they love you today, I love you and God does too.

~COFFEE WITH GOD~

This morning I asked God if everyone has a purpose? He said, "Son, everyone has a purpose, and anyone can change your thought, your day, or your life. Even a brief meeting with someone can become a significant part of your future, it may be positive or negative, or it can be a small piece of the puzzle. Life is like a puzzle, every little piece will become part of the big picture and the big picture is My plan for you.

Son, the choices you make can change everything in your life, or someone else's life. Everything that is negative doesn't always have a positive solution, but keeping positive thoughts and prayer can show others the picture is bigger than you can imagine so make the right choices and be a part of the big picture". Remember love is just a word until you put it between you and I, so if nobody has told you they love you today, I love you and God does too.

~COFFEE WITH GOD~

This morning I thought I would give you a tool for your box. Have you ever had an argument or a discussion with someone on the phone and they just hang up on you? Well try God, he will never hang up on you.

Sometime you may find a blank page in this book, please use it to write down your feelings, use it to write a message to a loved one who has passed. Please use that blank page or space to write God a message, use it to write a grateful list.

~COFFEE WITH GOD~

This morning I asked God about prayer. He said, "Son, just talk to me like you do, anytime and anywhere, I will always listen. Even when you don't know what to say, I know what you need".

Prayer doesn't always mean you're asking for something, you can always tell God what's on your mind when others won't listen.

He said "Prayer will help you keep balance in your life and it's the most powerful tool in your tool box. Some of the most popular prayer requests involve asking for health, courage, guidance and strength, or forgiveness and the occasional lottery number request". God smiled and said, "Sorry son I don't do the gambling requests, life is already a gamble when you don't bet on me".

Prayer doesn't have to be a ritual thing, let it be a natural thing. Remember love is just a word until you put it between you and I, so if nobody has told you they love you today, I love you and God does too.

~COFFEE WITH GOD~

This morning I asked God about "*Coffee with God*". He said, "Son, *Coffee with God* is how you start your day, you share our talks and inspirations with others. Those that know you know of Me. It has made your love for family, friends and life your happiness.

Our relationship is greater than it has ever been and you have found faith and trust in me. Sharing this with others has allowed others to find their way also".

When I realized my life was changing for the better I knew God had always been with me, I just didn't know how to talk to Him. If you haven't found a way to talk to God, please do.   Remember love is just a word until you put it between you and I, so if nobody has told you they love you today, I love you and God does too.

~COFFEE WITH GOD~

This morning I asked God about resentments. He said, "Son, resentments are like anchors, they will slow you down and even stop you from moving on in life. Resentments can make life seem like you're in a hostage situation, and may cause you to not love, not care, or even lose some of the values of life. Resentments eat you from within and like a cancer, destroy relationships with the ones you love and the ones who love you.

There may be others in your life who will hold on to your past and at any given time bring up old tensions. Son, you have made many mistakes in your life and many have affected the lives of your friends and your family.

You must first forgive yourself, and make amends or ask for forgiveness from others, this will help you to move on in life. Son, asking me to forgive you is the easy part, forgiving yourself is the hard part. No one deserves to be a hostage, life is too short, so learn to let go".

Remember love is just a word until you put it between you and I, so if nobody has told you they love you today, I love you and God does too.

COFFEE WITH GOD~

This morning I asked God who am I? He said, "Son, you are a child of mine and in this world you are somebody. Be careful of the choices you make because someone is always there to judge you. Know I love you and I will always lead you to make the right choices. Only you can make your own decisions". Remember love is just a word until you put it between you and I, so if nobody has told you they love you today, I love you and God does too.

~COFFEE WITH GOD~

This morning I asked God should I go to work?   He said, "Son, you don't have to go to work, you can just lay there and expect nothing in your life, or you can get up and do something.

Know that success is not of material things, but of the values in your life. Even if you're not working, get up and do something positive, if not for yourself do something positive for someone else. When you do this, don't expect a reward or pay. The payoff, is knowing someone may be grateful.

Just know you have made a long term investment. Life is just like any job,   you do your job and you get paid for your services. The payoff in life is doing unto others as you want others to do unto you.

Son, if you do the right things, the right things will happen which includes going to work.   Consider *"Coffee with God"* a long term investment, because sharing is caring and people are grateful for your work".

Remember love is just a word until you put it between you and I, so if nobody has told you they love you today, I love you and God does too.

T.G.I.F. =TRUSTING GOD IS FAITH

~COFFEE WITH GOD~

This morning I asked God about the bad people in my life. He said, "Son, there will be good and bad people in your life. The good are obviously meaningful and grateful to have you in their lives. The bad will show you all the things you don't want or need in life, so choose your friends wisely". If nobody has told you they love you today, I do and God does too.

~COFFEE WITH GOD~

This morning I asked God about life. He said, "Son, life is not a game but a reality. In it there will be people who love you and others who will treat you without care.   In life it's not how you're treated, it's how you react to it which will determine how far you go in life.

Don't let the inner workings of society or others lead you in the wrong direction.   Everyday things will happen that make you stop and think, that's why life is a learning experience, so you don't have to react to everything.   Don't be surprised at what others will do, be amazed at all the good you can do.

When you wake up in the morning and you look in the mirror and smile, this means you are somebody. That's a reality, keep love in your heart and have hate for no one". Remember love is just a word until you put it between you and I, so if nobody has told you they love you today, I love you and God does too.

~COFFEE WITH GOD~

This morning I asked God about my future. He said, "Son, your future has already started by the decisions you make, the love you have in your life and the motivation you have to share and tell others you love them.

Your past is now the wisdom of your future, don't dwell on the small details of yesterday. Everything happens for a reason. Don't become discouraged when things don't happen right away.

In the past you became impatient or frustrated, this was before you found faith and trust in Me. Now you have hope, you know anything is possible for your future. Son, never forget where you have been, your uncomfortable past is only a memory and it doesn't have to be a part of your future".

You know you're having a great day when God wakes you up and it doesn't matter which side of the bed you wake up on. Remember love is just a word until you put it between you and I, so if nobody has told you they love you today, I love you and God does too.

~Understanding the dreams of others may sometimes conflict with friendships in life. Reality is in check and God will always reveal to those in the dark, what self has discovered with His light… your foundation is only as strong as your faith and with faith, hope never dies. Wishing you well and God Bless!

T.G.I.F. =TODAYS GIFT IS FREEDOM

~INSPIRATION~

Having a father in your life is a blessing; if he is also a father figure then you have a gift. It's one thing to be a father, it's a great thing to be the man in a child's life...be responsible and take care of your children, it's never too late. I have the two greatest fathers of all time, God and my dad Lou...I love you dad!

If ever in life you think you have too much on your plate...act like you're at a BBQ and get another plate.

When you look at yourself in the mirror you should be able to smile!

~INSPIRATION~

The A.R.T. that will ENABLE your life

ACCOUNTABLE

RESPONSIBLE

TRUSTABLE

~COFFEE WITH GOD~

This morning I asked God about life changers. He said, "Son, every day is a new day, a new way of life. Yesterday is now a part of your past and you found you have been blessed again when I woke you this morning.

Looking back on all you experienced and learned from yesterday, it may help you get through your new day. Some people can wake each day, and may not realize it's a new day, because they will continue to dwell on the past.

Putting life in perspective, you have grown to realize each day something or someone new can come into your life and change things forever, a life changer. Son, this is part of one of the many journeys in your life, keep hope in your life and love in your heart".

Friendships can start with togetherness, so if we walk together, we can talk together, and when we meet together we can eat together, most of all, if we pray together, we can stay together.

Remember love is just a word until you put it between you and I, so if nobody has told you they love you today, I love you and God does too.

~INSPIRATION~

One of the hardest things you will have to do is learn to forgive yourself.   You have done things that continue to hold your mind hostage. Forgive yourself and give them to God. One day at a time will help you to understand and learn from your mistakes and the mistakes of others.

~COFFEE WITH GOD~

This morning I asked God about greed. He said, "Son, all through life you will have many choices, you won't always make the right decisions, but learn from your mistakes. Any decision you make, can and will affect those around you and sometimes your future. Don't make choices that involve greed, or if the end result is at the expense of others. Greed is often a result of wanting more than I bless you with, or because of the need to feed your ego or an addiction.

Son, greed is a choice and sometimes the end result may have a bad outcome. Don't be tempted by the shining star, just appreciate the glow of the moon and know beyond any star that can be seen, there are blessings that can't be seen. For many it's hard to believe if you do the right thing the right things will happen. Never let greed or your ego get in the way of making the right decisions" Remember love is just a word until you put it between you and I, so if nobody has told you they love you today, I love you and God does too.

~INSPIRATION~

Every day for the rest of your life you will be reminded of your past, the good, the bad and the ugly and those are the characters of your life. You have learned from each of them and now you have turned your life over to God and have become one person, with character. Love and respect of yourself and others has made you someone with a future.

~COFFEE WITH GOD~

This morning I asked God about change. He said, "Son, if you're doing something which is conflicting with your living conditions, it's time to change.

Begin each day with prayer, which is always a good place to start. There will be some things you will want in life, many will be material things and they may cloud your focus on the more important things in life.

Sometimes an obsession will take over and soon you may find yourself in an uncomfortable situation resulting from clouded judgments. Trying to find the answer to life's problems isn't in the material things of life, you will find material things are only a temporary fix.

Some will hit rock bottom and realize it's time to change, some won't and as they go down they will take you with them. Spending quality time with family and friends may help you to understand you don't always need to have material things just to feel good about yourself.

Son, if you want a better way of life, turn your life around and change". I did, and now, I have been clean and sober since June 2007 and my life is Rantastic! Remember love is just a word until you put it between you and I, so if nobody has told you they love you today, I love you and God does too.

~INSPIRATION~

You will meet a lot of people in your life and each one can teach one, no matter bad or good. Things can be learned from any and all. The unseen can be sought, the unspoken can be heard, the lost can be found and the misguided can be forgiven. Life is a reality and the truth can be a learning experience.

~COFFEE WITH GOD~

This morning I asked God about "Just because". He said, "Son, sometimes things aren't always as they appear, but don't give up on your dreams just because you think things aren't going your way. Do not become discouraged, prayer along with faith and trust in Me will always get you through it.

Family and friends may try to be there for you, and sometimes they can't be there, for some reason or another, or maybe it's just because. Son, just because it doesn't happen when you want it to, remember it is My will that will put you were you need to be, when you need to be.

Son, I am always with you, even when it seems you may have lost your direction. I will never lead you wrong and just because you can't see Me, doesn't mean I am not here with you". Remember love is just a word until you put it between you and I, so if nobody has told you they love you today, I love you and God does too.

~COFFEE WITH GOD~

This morning I spoke with God and He told me to share this with you. He said, "Son, there have been many who have sacrificed their lives, time with family and friends, holidays, and everyday living conditions.

There have been many brave, courageous, unselfish, and dedicated men and women who have served in the United States Armed Forces so you can have the freedoms you have now. They have been a part of your past and have sacrificed for your future, and they never give up.

So when possible, take the time to pay respect and honor those who have fallen before and the ones who still stand. Shake their hand and give a hug to the ones who have done their duty, served and sacrificed".

Thank you for having the courage to do, what I didn't have the courage to do. We should pay our respects to the service men and women of this country. To the service men and women of this nation, past, present, and future I thank you for your service, it is greatly appreciated. Remember love is just a word until you put it between you and I, so if nobody has told you they love you today, I love you and God does too.

~COFFEE WITH GOD~

This morning I asked God about acceptance. He said, "Son, as you go through life, you will find every day will be an experience, and you will have days with ups and downs. You will meet people from all walks of life, some will treat you with respect, and some won't give you the time of day.

At times, someone may say something you just don't want to hear, and sometimes without thought, you may want to lash out. Sometimes you will be told things you don't want to hear, but maybe you need to listen.

Son, things don't always have to happen as you plan, the most important thing is you understand and have acceptance that your life is what you make of it. Change what you can and accept what you can't, pray to know the difference. Don't let the inner workings of others bring you down, and know I am always with you.

Son, remember with faith, hope never dies and you don't have to experience bad days alone. If you have trust in Me you won't have any bad days, maybe a bad moment, but no more bad days" Remember love is just a word until you put it between you and I, so if nobody has told you they love you today, I love you and God does too.

~COFFEE WITH GOD~

This morning I want to share with you that I thank God every day. I used to think I'm not supposed to be alive. There were days I used to think nobody cared and I didn't matter.

I found out that if I wasn't a part of God's plan, I wouldn't be here and neither would you. If you are reading this that means God has guided you to a place to make you realize you are worth it. You can have a positive change in your life at any time and pay it forward by sharing an inspiration or a blessing to anyone, at any time.

Prayer, faith, and trust in God are three of the tools I use, to do the right things in my life now. Sharing God's love is my way of paying it forward, I know I am truly a part of His plan and He loves me. Tell someone you love them today. Remember love is just a word until you put it between you and I, so if nobody has told you they love you today, I love you and God does too.

You are somebody and thank you for being a part of my life and my recovery/renovation!

~COFFEE WITH GOD~

This morning I asked God about success. He said, "Son, success is when you never give up, things you want in life can, or will become material, material things don't make you successful.

What you do with your life will determine if you will be successful, when it's not at the expense of others. Sharing, caring, and love of others make you a success.

You will never know when it is your time, but knowing you never gave up, that's when it can be said you were successful". Remember love is just a word until you put it between you and I, so if nobody has told you they love you today, I love you and God does too.

~COFFEE WITH GOD~

This morning I would like to dedicate this time and post to the men and women of this country, past and present, who have given their time, efforts, and heart for the well being, freedom, health and welfare of this nation.

As from the tragedy, and the ones who sacrificed their lives, on September 11, 2001. The ones who have suffered health problems, as a result of their efforts to help, and aid in the search and rescue of any possible survivors from the attack.

September 11, 2001 is a day that will live in the minds of many and will be heartfelt forever. The events of that day affected the whole planet in one way or another and we still feel the pain and suffer the ever lasting effects from that day.

To the families of those who serve, and have served this country, the hardship and the sleepless nights not knowing how your loved ones are doing.

This is also for the parent or parents who can't witness the birth, the first steps, the first words or the first day of school because you found it important to serve our country and protect our land and this nation, known as the United States of America.

There are no words great enough to say how much you are appreciated and loved. I give you the utmost respect and highest regard as a human being...I thank you with a handshake, a hug and I'm honored to call each and every one of you "My hero"! Remember love is just a word until you put it between you and I, so if nobody has told you they love you today, I love you and God does too.

~COFFEE WITH GOD~

This morning I asked God about apologizing or making amends. He said, "Son, making amends or apologizing is a sign of integrity and courage from within your heart. Some people will think it's a sign of weakness, but when they have that thought, it's because their ego has gained control of their integrity.

Son, keep in mind during this process, some people can't let things go and more accusations of other things may arise or they want to make you feel more guilt. This is when you need to be strong and accept that making mistakes is a part of life and making amends is how you get through life.

Pray before you make a leap of faith is always a good idea. Making amends and apologizing means you can learn from your mistakes and show you have integrity and you care and respect yourself and others.

Son, you can learn from others but you can also learn from yourself, and remember, history will repeat itself when you make the same mistakes and you don't learn from them". Three more words you should put in your tool box… "I am sorry". Remember love is just a word until you put it between you and I, so if nobody has told you they love you today, I love you and God does too.

~COFFEE WITH GOD~

This morning I asked God about obstacles. He said, "Son, when you decided to turn your life around you had many things which tried to defeat you, you only changed lanes and not direction. You can have a bad moment, but you don't have any bad days.

There were people who you associated with telling you that you would be back, and others said you wouldn't make it. All through life there will be people who will doubt you, who want you to fail, or will try and kick you because they think you are down.

You have made things seem possible to others, you have achieved things which seemed impossible and you have made many family and friends proud because you never gave up. The obstacles you thought were mountains were only speed bumps, the waters you thought were too deep, you built a bridge and got over them.

Son, there will always be obstacles in your life, but never give up". To anyone who reads this please don't ever give up on your recovery, your life or your dreams…with prayer anything is possible. Remember love is just a word until you put it between you and I, so if nobody has told you they love you today, I love you and God does too.

~COFFEE WITH GOD~

This morning I asked God about recovery. He said, "Son, sometimes getting into recovery is like joining a gang, you get a beat down before you get in.

Things you learn in recovery will become the tools of life, and you can learn how to live without putting mind altering substances in your body to face life on life's terms. Things will happen in your life the same as it happens in the lives of others, the solution can become available to an unaltered mind and all things shall pass with prayer.

It's unfortunate some people start off trying to be a weekend warrior and eventually they find that Monday never comes. Every day is an experience and lessons can be learned, they don't have to be learned the hard way. Many have tried to do it alone and find the only thing they are good at doing alone is digging a deeper hole. Have faith and trust in Me, remember that I am always just a prayer away".

Remember love is just a word until you put it between you and I, so if nobody has told you they love you today, I love you and God does too.

~COFFEE WITH GOD~

This morning I asked God about hope. He said, "Son, sometimes life doesn't seem like its fair, but you should know each day will be different. Every day you can wake up with a new outlook on life, just by having hope, a good attitude, and no expectations of others.

You may learn to control your thoughts, emotions, decisions, and most of all your actions. It's so important to keep your head and your heart in what you want out of life.

Daily decisions are made in everyone's life and some will affect you, this is why you should not judge others and have no expectations. Son, know this, I walk with you every step of your day no matter what. When you want to change your life, do the right thing and the right things will happen, and remember with faith, hope never dies". Remember love is just a word until you put it between you and I, so if nobody has told you they love you today, I love you and God does too.

~COFFEE WITH GOD~

This morning I asked God about GPS. He said, "Son, the road to hell is paved with good intentions and the bridge to expectations can be deceiving. These are some of the things you will learn in life and often they can be a painful or heartbreaking experience.

Don't be discouraged by the obstacles you meet in life, even when they are the result of a choice you made. Mistakes can and will be made, although your intentions were meant for the best, don't always expect a favorable outcome.

In life there will be people you can depend on and they may have the best intentions and sometimes things will happen. Keep your head up and your heart in it, and know I will always be here for you. Prayer is the best answer to any doubt you may have".

I now know GPS means two things…"God plants and seeds", because I'm growing, and it also means, "God points and steers", because my life is headed in the right direction. Remember love is just a word until you put it between you and I, so if nobody has told you they love you today, I love you and God does too.

~COFFEE WITH GOD~

This morning I asked God about turning the page.
He said, "Son, there are people in your life, that think
they have the right of way in your life. In time you
grow to realize everything is not as it appears and it
can be your expectations that led you there.

Mistakes happen and you learn to move on and try to
look at things in a different way, by not judging or
planting aliases on others. Son, you must understand
and accept that some will not be able to turn the
page on your mistakes or the mistakes of themselves,
even after making amends. This is when resentments
will raise its presence and bad things may come from
this.

I know it's not always a fair shake even when you
have tried to turn the page, but let it go son, and have
faith and trust I will take care of you". Remember
love is just a word until you put it between you and I,
so if nobody has told you they love you today, I love
you and God does too.

~COFFEE WITH GOD~

This morning I asked God about understanding others. He said, "Son, as you walk through life you will meet many people from all different walks of life. Many of them will just pass through your life and never be seen again, know this was a chance meeting. Some may become friends, maybe just for a brief moment in your life but none the less they have now become a part of your life. The ones who continue to be a part of your life will have meaning and you may become life changers for each other.

Son, accepting others in your life is one thing, if you try to understand everyone, this can become exhausting. Sometimes you're not meant to understand someone, but understanding yourself is a part of life you must learn.

Know someone is always watching you and some will judge you and not even know you. You can accept life and the people you meet or you can go through life trying to understand everyone you meet and miss out on your own life".

Remember love is just a word until you put it between you and I, so if nobody has told you they love you today, I love you and God does too.

Some people have come and gone in my life, I thank God you are not one of them.

~COFFEE WITH GOD~

This morning I asked God about, "Before it's too late". He said, "Son, from the time you are born you will have people who love you, and really care about your future. As life goes on you get to know the people who knew you before you were born, and you may become a part of their life and they may become a part of yours.

Distance may soon develop between your existences, yet you still have a mutual bond called life and still, they knew you before you were born. Every once in a while you see each other at events or in passing, maybe even at a family gathering, smiles, laughs and memories are exchanged, and yet they knew you before you were born.

Time passes and as you get older, families get greater, and so does the distance between visits, don't let this become the reason you forget someone who knew you before you were born. Son, everyone has a time and tomorrow is never promised, that's why you always say, "I love you".

Don't wait a lifetime to say those words before it's too late". Those who know me and my family know we share those words with you and we always will. Remember love is just a word until you put it between you and I, so if nobody has told you they love you today, I love you and God does too.

This is not just about people who knew you before you were born, God also knew you before you were born, so read this again and now put God in those places you may have been thinking of (people), someone who knew you before you were born.

~COFFEE WITH GOD~

This morning I asked God about redemption. He said, "Son, everyone in life will make mistakes, some more serious than others. In one way or another you will make mistakes which will affect someone else's life, the reality of this is that mistakes will always affect more than just one person. Some will forgive and some won't but the important thing is you learn from your mistakes and strive to redeem yourself.

Having an understanding of yourself and what it means to be accountable will help you in your growth and the progress you make from day to day. Having an open mind and having no expectations of others as you strive to redeem yourself, is known as progress rather than perfection.

Son, this is the time in your life you now call renovation, rebuilding your foundation and deleting the bad immoral ideas of the life you had been a part of for so long. Some will come to see you as a responsible human being with a high level of integrity and honesty in your life.

Unfortunately, son, not everyone will appreciate and admire your efforts, but it's not for them to control your redemption or your progress.   Make amends with your past and mature as a responsible person will have family and friends respecting your efforts to become a changed person, and son this is a tool known as redemption". Remember love is just a word until you put it between you and I, so if nobody has told you they love you today, I love you and God does too.

~COFFEE WITH GOD~

This morning I asked God about saying goodbye. He said, "Son, saying goodbye is like the end of the show or the end of the road. Even in life you will have people come and go, good and bad, but do you really want to say goodbye?

Changing who you are means also changing how you treat others and not being judgmental. Even if you don't care to have them in your life, pray for them and hope one day to see them as a better person, remember son, maybe you used to be that person.

Letting go of the bitterness or the resentments you may have against one or more persons in your life is something you can say goodbye to, a disease or a bad job is something you can say goodbye to.

Son, anyone you meet in life, bad, good, sharing or not caring, don't say goodbye just say see you later and always leave them with a thought in your mind and a prayer in your heart".

Remember love is just a word until you put it between you and I, so if nobody has told you they love you today, I love you and God does too.

~COFFEE WITH GOD~

This morning I thanked God for allowing me to find out who I really am. I can really appreciate the blessings I have in my life, including the gifts of family and friends whom I love so very much.

It's this time of the year when many devastating things can happen in the life of an active addict or alcoholic and this is the time of year we can take the most from family and friends, and not just material things, we also steal time from loved ones and I do remember those days.

It's this time of year we should all reach out to the people in our lives and let them know how much they are loved. A positive way of life can start right here and now, by letting go of the past and moving on to a brighter, promising future. No matter how things may look, God is always on our side.

Don't wait for the New Year to make resolutions, this is thanksgiving and we all should learn to give thanks to those around us, the good, the bad and the ugly and we have all been a part of that type of life.

It's time to give thanks and make a change, have a safe holiday and if nobody has told you they love you today, I do and God does too!

~COFFEE WITH GOD~

This morning I asked God about four letter words. He said, "Son, there will be a lot of four letter words in your life but there are two words which will stand out in your mind every day in your life.

The first word is "hate", and this word has no use in the life of someone who wants a better way of life. Sometimes it's used in a joking way and yet it is a hurtful word with no joking foundations. It is expressed, sometimes people have no idea or just don't care the impact it can have on another human being. Hate is such a strong word and has such negative meaning.

The other four letter word in your life is "love", and it has a strong foundation. You will find if you base your life on the foundation of love you can find much happiness in life with family and friends. Although hate is all around you, you don't need to participate in the actions of others who wish to have hate in their life.

The love you have for others will always be appreciated by someone in your life and you may never know, but telling someone "I love you" can have a positive and lasting effect on the world around you". I hope you have a great and beautiful day, remember love is just a word until you put it between you and I, so if nobody has told you they love you today, I love you and God does too.

~COFFEE WITH GOD~

This morning I asked God about getting high. He said, "Son, back when everything in your life seemed like it wasn't going your way, you found an escape with drugs or alcohol. This was only a temporary fix and only made for more pain and suffering for you and others.

Many times you felt the world was against you and you never thought to try and find a solution to your problems. So you turned to a mind altering substance to temporarily mask the problems by getting high.

Son, now that you have turned your life around, you have found more rewarding ways to get high. When your grandkids tell you they love you, when your family and friends tell you they are proud of you and how you have changed to become a better person, some won't understand this is how you get high now.

Some won't understand the impact of the trust you have built and the responsibilities you now take care of in your life. Your faith and trust in Me is why you have happiness in your life.

Son, some won't understand this is how you get high today, but if you share with them the love and the blessings and pray for them maybe others can learn to get high the same way you do". Remember love is just a word until you put it between you and I, so if nobody has told you they love you today, I love you and God does too.

~COFFEE WITH GOD~

This morning I asked God about "What if"? He said, "Son, thinking about where you have been, what you have done, and who you have met in your life is no accident. There's always going to be that question throughout your life, your curiosity will always exist and you will often dwell on it.

When you get to the point in your life where you continue to look back and think things could have been different, realize this…it would have been different…if.

Son, the past is the past and it cannot be changed, it can be relived throughout the rest of your life, but it may soon become a resentment. If you have great memories you love to keep close at heart, that's fine. If you have memories of bad times, consider those experiences and let those be the lessons you've learned and move on.

Everybody has times in their life they won't ever forget, and it's often followed up with a "what if" moment. In your "what if" moment, things could have either been a great decision or a bad decision…fact is son, you will never know, learn to move on". Remember love is just a word until you put it between you and I, so if nobody has told you they love you today, I love you and God does too.

~COFFEE WITH GOD~

This morning I asked God about having a heart. He said, "Son, it's not how big your heart is, it's what's in your heart that has meaning in your life.

It's when you can see past imperfections and look at the beauty of a person, and know there is no such perfection. When you know the world around you and the people in it don't always share the same thoughts or the same beliefs, you still have love for them. Respect yourself even though you have character defects and short comings, you still treat others with respect and care.

Son, you may think the world has much hate in it and you may experience some parts of it every day, but realize this, it's not hate, it's a fear of the unknown and for people who have a closed mind and a lost soul.

It takes courage to accept others for who and what they are, but son it takes a heart to love someone you don't even know or even someone you have never met in person. Look past the imperfections of others and have a heart". Remember love is just a word until you put it between you and I, so if nobody has told you they love you today, I love you and God does too.

~COFFEE WITH GOD~

This morning I asked God about touching lives. He said, "Son, everything you will ever do in your life, every person you will ever meet, or any place you will ever go, sometimes nothing can mean more than when you touch the life of another.

In your lifetime, you have the ability to change the life of another at any given time, on any given day. You may change someone's life by being a positive influence, giving someone a much needed pat on the back, speaking words of encouragement or giving someone a helping hand.

You can make someone feel they have a purpose just by letting them know you really do care, by speaking to that person who seems to have no one to turn to. By reaching out and sharing a smile and a hug at a meeting.

Remember handshakes are for business deals, hugs are for saving lives. Son, some people just don't care and they show it by being inconsiderate or having no respect for others. Somewhere, somehow, this type of person may find out life will only have meaning when they learn to care about life itself and the others around them.

Son, remember the only time you look down at someone is when you're helping them up." I hope you find that life has more meaning when you have love and care for others. Remember love is just a word until you put it between you and I, so if nobody has told you they love you today, I love you and God does too.

~COFFEE WITH GOD~

This morning I asked God about changing my life. He said, "Son, there comes a time in a person's life when they realize in order to be somebody you have to change your life.

At some point you may have thought the important things in life were material things, having wads of money in your pocket, a nice car with a bumpin' sound system, or wearing a pair of $100 shoes just to go and buy a bottle and a pack of cigarettes from the corner liquor store.

You may even have thought it was really cool to walk around with your pants sagging, because you saw a few others doing it. Fact is, at one point in your life you thought it was ok to talk loudly and cuss in public places, all because you wanted attention.

Maybe there was a time when you went to a fast food place or a store and your service wasn't "celebrity status", so you thought it was ok to make a scene and rant about the poor service.

Son, there comes a time when you need to realize in order to be respected, you must first give respect. In order to be loved, you must first love, and in order to be something in life, you must first be somebody in life.

A blind person can't see the material things in life, they only hear and feel what life is about, and sometimes that is all you need to be somebody". Remember love is just a word until you put it between you and I, so if nobody has told you they love you today, I love you and God does too.

~COFFEE WITH GOD~

This morning I would like to share with everyone this weekend was a meaningful weekend. Some people will learn how to be grateful for family, friends, and life itself. Some will come to understand the meaning of giving rather than receiving, being humble and not being egotistical.

Many will be with family and friends and come to understand one of the most important feelings in life will be the experience of love. Unfortunately, there are many who won't get to experience the feeling of warmth, family, giving or even receiving. It's also unfortunate many don't know how to share, experience, or even show love around this time of year without putting a mind altering substance in their body.

It is especially this time of year we need to realize in order to experience the Love, we have to be able to show the Love. So if you think you must have some mind altering substance in your body, try to be grateful and experience the love before you go there.

This will be my 5th Christmas and New Year without the use of drugs and alcohol in my body and each year it gets better. I won't have the money to give presents like I have in the past, but I will be able to give a hug and say Merry Christmas, Happy New Year and I love you. I thank God he allows me to experience life with a clear mind and a warm heart. I hope you have a great day and if nobody has told you they love you today, I do and God does too.

~COFFEE WITH GOD~

This morning I asked God about my dreams. He said, "Son, there is proof around you to know if you work hard enough and you really want to make something positive out of your life, dreams may come true.

Sometimes there will be obstacles which seem like they have no other purpose but to discourage you from your focus. There will be people who want nothing more than to keep you from your dreams. Don't hate or judge them, pray for them and hope someday they will have positive dreams as well.

Keep your focus on the road and the journey ahead, there will be many forks in your road but the directions can be found in your tool box.

Maintaining a balance in your life will help you to continue in your achievements, make a schedule and set your plans in action by not straying from your goals. Pray for courage, guidance, and strength and always have hope for your future.

Son, remember with faith, hope never dies". Remember love is just a word until you put it between you and I, so if nobody has told you they love you today, I love you and God does too.

~COFFEE WITH GOD~

This morning I asked God about change and time. He said, "Son, there are many different times in your life and you only have control of the present.

As you were growing up someone may have had control over the things you did and the time you were able to do them. You may or may not have been ok with the decisions someone else made for you, but in time this would change.

As you grew older sometimes you were able to make your own decisions, but maybe someone was also a part of your decision making. Now you're older and you feel times have changed and you're able to make your own decisions.

You look back in time and realize sometimes you didn't make the right decisions. These are the lessons you learned from your past and can be called experience. It's ok to admit you made mistakes in your past, that's called being accountable.

You have the choice to make your own decisions today and that's called being responsible. Son, one thing you must learn is you can't change time but you can change things in time, progress takes time and change is a part of that". Remember love is just a word until you put it between you and I, so if nobody has told you they love you today, I love you and God does too.

~COFFEE WITH GOD~

This morning I asked God about spirit. He said, "Son, in most everyone there is a drive to want to be someone, to be understood and to be loved. There is a part of you that wants the ability to make someone smile, and to know you have been an inspiration in at least one person's life.

As you go through your journey in life, you meet people with different beliefs, personalities, some open minded, some not so open minded. The important thing is you have the ability to share your spirit and the love which has been instilled in you, and this may show others life is more than just status in society.

When you have spirit, your happiness is constant, and your positive emotions can be shared by many. Son, you have devoted your life to sharing inspirations and spreading your blessings and your constant happiness. This is a true indication of faith and hope in your life and many now share your faith and hope, this is the gift you have made from the blessings you have received and now it's obvious to many you have a positive spirit within you".

Today I love who I am because I have found God in my life, and through faith and hope I have found a spirit you can find also, you just have to believe and trust in him. Remember love is just a word until you put it between you and I, so if nobody has told you they love you today, I love you and God does too.

~COFFEE WITH GOD~

This morning I asked God about two sided stories. He said, "Son, no matter what you do in life, someone is always going to talk about you. No matter how much you try to be a good person, someone will find a fault in you. No matter what your side of the story is, their side will always be different and it might seem unfair, but there are two sides to every story.

Don't feed into the frenzy of chaos, don't continue to try and find blame in others and don't fall into the negative wave of conversation. Words can be harmful in many ways, when said in certain tones or when told in an unfavorable way, you're made out to be someone of no respect.

Son its ok, there are other things in life to be more concerned with aside from the two sides to every story. Things might be said in a very degrading way but life goes on and there is always redemption. You can still have love in your heart, and even through acceptance, you can learn to forgive the other side of the story.

Son, I will bring light to what appears to be in the dark, the most important thing is to not judge by the criticism, don't judge by the side you haven't heard, and don't dwell on the unknown. This is not a perfect world and no one is without fault, but with prayer, two sides can become one". Have a great day and don't worry someone is always talking about you, just don't dwell on it. Remember love is just a word until you put it between you and I, so if nobody has told you they love you today, I love you and God does too.

~COFFEE WITH GOD~

This morning I would like to thank each and every one of you for all the love and support you have given me with, "*Coffee with God*". I have been blessed and inspired by your comments and the "like" responses I get on my morning posts of *CWG*.

It is my hope many will realize from my messages, we all have a purpose in life and each one can teach one. I have been through a lot in my life and being clean and sober since June 2007 has shown me when you decide to turn your life around, you can have a positive effect on the people you come in contact with.

I have learned how to use the tools I have been given in my years of recovery and they have helped me to overcome some moments of unrest. God has allowed me to become a responsible, accountable, and loved human being who once was not allowed in my parents' home without an escort.

God has blessed me with the gift to share inspirations which might help others overcome moments of unrest and doubt. I love who I am today because I decided to turn my life around and even when there was doubt, I did the best thing I knew which was pray.

I talk to God all day every day and I don't have any more bad days. I might have a bad moment, but no more bad days. It has been proven to me with faith, hope never dies. I never look down on anyone unless I'm helping them up, and I never have to put a mind altering substance in my body to be somebody.

Remember love is just a word until you put it between you and I, so if nobody has told you they love you today, I love you and God does too.

~COFFEE WITH GOD~

This morning I asked God about coming together. He said, "Son, fresh new things are possible for anyone who wants a new way of life or to just simply renovate their life. It is possible many won't realize how wonderful life is, while they can't appreciate up, until they have been down.

You have learned how to plant your seeds, and now you can reap what you have sown. Last year at this time you had no idea where your life would be one year later, but you hoped it would be enriched and blessed with promise.

Even if you have made some bad choices, you have planted positive people in your life and planted your positive way of life around others. This is an expression and a way to show love for life, and the respect, love, and care of others.

Son, continue to do the positive things you have done to achieve your happiness and the goals you wish to reach and you will find yourself there one day.

Never give up on your dreams, always remember you have tools to work with to maintain a good balance in life. These are how and why your life is coming together and son, I'm always just a prayer away". Remember love is just a word until you put it between you and I, so if nobody has told you they love you today, I love you and God does too.

~COFFEE WITH GOD~

This morning I asked God about resolutions. He said, "Son, I walk with you everyday side by side, and no walk is too far, no distance is too great and I would never abandon you.

Every day someone will vow to make a change in their life, maybe stop doing something harmful or maybe start doing something to become healthy. It won't matter if you try or not, if your heart isn't in it, there is no hope. If you don't believe in yourself, there is no faith. When you choose to build a foundation on your future, choose a road which will allow you to reach your goals and not a road where there are many obstacles marked, "I gave up here".

Don't always rely on encouragement from others, it won't always be there. There will always be someone who wishes the best for you, they might appear supportive and they probably mean well, but somehow you rely on that support to keep you going and it won't always be there.

Son, building a foundation in your life is very important when you are trying to change for the better. Make sure you have a plan and write it down, start a checklist and stick to it. Son, I walk with you every day and even when the sun doesn't shine in your day, my light will lead your way. Even when it seems like the darkest of the hour, pray for courage, guidance, and strength and I shall lead you through it". Remember love is just a word until you put it between you and I, so if nobody has told you they love you today, I love you and God does too.

~COFFEE WITH GOD~

This morning I asked God about giants. He said, "Son, when you become a part of a positive population of people, you stand tall and you become a giant. The life you, your family, and friends experience is based on the positive aura and affects you put out and have around you. Other people will look at that, some will ask how can they enrich their lives and find the same kind of happiness.

Son, you, and the positive people around you become giants and you see far because you stand on the shoulders of giants. Those who inspire you, those you inspire, and the display of care and love helps many. You may never know the impact you can have just by being humble, and paying it forward.

Son, remember you didn't get to where you are in life right now by yourself, with the help of the giants in your life you learned how to ask for help, how to learn from your mistakes, how to teach and not preach and how to love and respect yourself first.

Sometimes in life you have to get a beat down before you can learn how to get back up and that climb is the tool you call perseverance. It may not be something you planned for it can just happen, when you recover and you share your experience, strength and hope in a positive way, you become somebody's giant". Remember love is just a word until you put it between you and I, so if nobody has told you they love you today, I love you and God does too.

~COFFEE WITH GOD~

This morning I asked God about getting it done. He said, "Son, after a time you develop a schedule or you learn how to plan out your day so things don't get complicated. It is a good idea to just write things down as you become more accountable and responsible, you will have more responsibilities. This is a part of life, and is necessary to maintain a balance in life in order to know your life is on the right track.

Even when things seem to clutter in life, all you have to do is slow down, and get it done, one task at a time. A person can only live one day at a time, so be patient with the daily routines you may encounter, it's your life and only you should control your decisions.

Projects can happen over the course of time, tasks can happen on a routine schedule, but life happens every day and when you start your day off with prayer everything else falls into place.

Son, the older you get, you will begin to ask yourself more often, "Where did the time go"? Time will fly when you're having fun, when you're with family and friends and when you know you made the right decision to renovate your life". Some people say you only live once, which is so far from the truth…you live every day, and every day you can add on to the renovation of your life. Remember love is just a word until you put it between you and I, so if nobody has told you they love you today, I love you and God does too.

~COFFEE WITH GOD~

This morning I asked God about situations in life. He said, "Son, there are many things you have learned in life and many more things you have learned in recovery, and the experiences and lessons are now tools in your tool box.

No matter what type of situations you are faced with in life now, you have a tool which will help you find a way to get through it. The important thing is no matter what, you know you don't have to resort to anything illegal, disrespecting, inconsiderate, or even deceptive just to provide you with a sense of satisfaction.

Times have not always been favorable, finances, employment, relationships, also friends and relatives either gone to soon or gone unexpectantly, these are things in life everyone will face at one time or another.

Your perseverance, acceptance, family and friends and most of all prayer will always help you through it. There will always be some who doubt or even question your intentions in life. Do the right thing and the right things will happen, as long as you believe in Me, I will always be here with you. Son, just because you can't see Me doesn't mean that I am not here". Remember love is just a word until you put it between you and I, so if nobody has told you they love you today, I love you and God does too.

~COFFEE WITH GOD~

This morning I asked God about my thoughts. He said, "Son, since you have a mind of your own and you know the difference between right and wrong, your mind won't always have pure and innocent thoughts.

All that you have been through and all you have seen in your life, it's just your mind and memory working together to form a thought. Not all thoughts have to be acted upon, you don't need to react to everything negative your mind visualizes for you.

You may have dreams of using a mind altering substance or having a drink, but it's simply your memory reliving an experience. You may wake up in the middle of the night or even after dozing off for a minute or so and believe you have actually done something against your will or something you may have never even thought about doing in your entire life. Pray on it son, go back to sleep, or get up and write about it. Let that be your reaction to your life's distraction.

Sometimes you might not be able to help what flashes in your mind at any given time, but you don't have to turn it into a bad moment. There are the tools of prayer and meditation which can often help reduce the amount of bad thoughts and dreams in your life". Remember love is just a word until you put it between you and I, so if nobody has told you they love you today, I love you and God does too.

~COFFEE WITH GOD~

This morning I asked God about how to start a good day? He said, "Son, every action will result in a reaction, from something or from someone. It's not how you're treated, it's how you react or respond to the situation that may or may not get you through it. So remember son, it's not how your treated, it's how you react to it which will make you a better person.

Sometimes it's just a good idea to think things through before you decide to make a decision you might regret. At the beginning of your day it's up to you to decide what kind of day you're going to have, and it's all in your attitude, your preparation, and prayer.

Keep in mind others around you will or may react to how you treat them, so even if your day isn't going great at first, it helps if you treat others in a positive way. Positive thoughts and positive actions could lead you in the right direction and this can be shared with others.

Keep happiness and love in your heart and a smile on your face and let the world know you are truly blessed and all because I woke you this morning, you prayed, thanked Me and started your day. Son, those are the tools to start a good day". Remember love is just a word until you put it between you and I, so if nobody has told you they love you today, I love you and God does too.

How did you start your day?

~COFFEE WITH GOD~

This morning I asked God about renovations. He said, "Son, now that you have turned your life around and you want only positive things in your life, there are other things you need to change also.

Becoming accountable and responsible is a big part, but you also have to do some renovations. Your foundation was based on deceit, manipulation, and the use of mind altering substances. During this time, you didn't care if you were on time, and you had no consideration of anyone else and their schedules.

You may have thought the world was supposed to wait on you or even cater to your needs, and you had no respect for yourself. Change and renovation can be subtle, and it doesn't have to be so drastic that it sends you right back out to the world of addiction.

Recovery is a process and you will find some people will look at you in a different, more respectable way now. You can now be proud of the person you have become, and it's all a part of your renovation process.

Son, you have created a positive aura and you have many family and friends who are now a part of your recovery. Don't ever stop your renovation process, and just keep moving forward, all the while you will appreciate the renovations you have made in your life". If you haven't started, now would be a good time to renovate your life. Remember love is just a word until you put it between you and I, so if nobody has told you they love you today, I love you and God does too.

~COFFEE WITH GOD~

This morning I want to share with you something that happened to me yesterday. I have not worked since before Thanksgiving, so money is extremely tight, but I went to the bank to withdraw money to pay my late rent.

As I approached the ATM I thought to myself, "I don't think I even have a dollar for the money order". I looked in my pocket for change and found a $5.00 bill, this made things fall into place. After pulling out the money at the ATM I walked over to Wal-Mart to get a money order.

As I stood in line, I reached in my pocket to count out the money and found I had lost the $5.00. Instead of getting mad, I smiled and said to myself I know God made that happen because whoever found it really needed the $5.00. So I got the money order for my rent (short $1.00) and as I walked back to my truck I tried to figure out how I lost the $5.00, felt around in my pockets with no luck.

I got home, went to the office to pay my rent, and shared with them what had just happened. Agreeing God gave it to a person who really needed it, I walked out with a smile. I went to my apartment to share the story with my roommate, agreeing God gave it to someone who really needed it, and then I went to take out the trash.

As I walked back to my apartment I reached in my pocket to get my keys and out falls a $5.00 bill, the very same one. God truly does have a sense of humor, because all along he knew I was the one who really needed the $5.00.

This shows me if I even still have care and love for others in my time of need, God will always have care and love in my time of need. Remember love is just a word until you put it between you and I, so if nobody has told you they love you today, I love you and God does too.

~COFFEE WITH GOD~

This morning I asked God about spreading the love. He said, "Son, the acts of kindness you perform throughout your life may add up, but it's the little gestures you do for others that can mean the most to someone.

When you take the time to ask a friend or even a stranger how they're doing, or even asking someone if they need help with something, that's a gesture of care. When you have people on Facebook who seem to always have drama on their page or drama in their life, you seem to reach out and offer a caring hand.

Not everyone knows how to pray and ask for courage, guidance, and strength, but you share how to have a relationship with Me through prayer and or meditation. It's not easy to try and convince or comfort someone when they don't have the faith you have, but son just being a caring person can make a difference.

Some people have trust issues and that's ok, it's just as easy to tell someone you don't want or need anything accept to pray for them. This is how you spread love by comforting with prayer and just being a friend in the times of need.

Son, not everyone has family and friends in their life and many will never get to experience the love, care and the happiness family and friends can bring to them. Just being in someone's life, if not but for just a brief moment, just know you may have left a positive influence just by spreading the love". Remember love is just a word until you put it between you and I, so if nobody has told you they love you today, I love you and God does too.

~COFFEE WITH GOD~

This morning I would like to again thank everyone for your love and support, its touches my heart to know there is love in the hearts of so many, and I am a part of it.

There have been many things which have happened in each and everyone's life, some were heartfelt, some will leave a lasting impression, but one of the greatest feelings is knowing you have spread Gods love and it is being shared with so many.

I have experienced the loss of 79 family and friends since 2004 and I have been clean and sober since June 2007. I will turn 51 years old in May 2013 and I have been around a lot of negative people and negative things in my life.

Just a normal life maybe, maybe not, but what I do know is when I finally found God in June 2007, my life turned around completely and I have found so many positive things about my life. I have many experiences and conversations I choose to share with you with the hope it lets you know life is what you make of it, but it can be even greater with God in your life.

The bottom line is this, whatever you and I did in our past, good, bad, or indifferent, no matter what it was, God has crossed our lives together and I truly believe we can help make this world a better place by spreading the love he has blessed us with.

When I write *"Coffee with God"*, I think of all of you and how it may help you through your day. I hope and pray each person who has been touched by one of my posts of CWG has decided they want a better way of life.

If we walk together we can talk together, if we meet together we can eat together and when we pray together we can stay together. Remember love is just a word until you put it between you and I, so if nobody has told you they love you today, I love you and God does too.

~COFFEE WITH GOD~

This morning I asked God about prospering. He said, "Son, there are a lot of things you may want in life, material things always come to mind. Window shopping in life may include a lot of things a person can feel are necessary to be happy.

It's ok to feel happy about how your life is going and it's ok to want some of the finer things in life. It's true when a person can start working and earning things they want to have the extras they couldn't have before. Just remember, sometimes material things can become a status symbol and for some it will begin to fuel their ego.

Son, this is not how you become prosperous, you become prosperous when you have love in your heart, you care for others, you reach out when you can and you never look down on anyone, unless you are helping them up, this is the life of a prosperous person.

You can enjoy some of the greater things in life like family and friends and spending quality time with those in need, even to make a phone call and just let someone know you were thinking about them. You can hold your head high and be proud you have turned your life around and you can stand tall and know you're doing the right things in life and this is the life of a prosperous person".

I pray you can learn to become prosperous in Gods way. Remember love is just a word until you put it between you and I, so if nobody has told you they love you today, I love you and God does too.

~COFFEE WITH GOD~

This morning I asked God about the plan. He said, "Son, all your family and friends whom you continue to have a relationship with, will continue to be just that family and friends. Other people who fall under the description of associates will still be in some way or another part of your life, maybe in memory or in passing.

The path each person decides to walk may be totally up to that person, and the one thing you should not have is expectations of others and the path they choose. Even throughout the daily obstacles in life, everyone will experience their own situations and use the tools they may have to get through it.

Son, you can suggest or even be of support for any family, friend or associate, but when someone makes a bad decision or even the tragedy at the loss of a life, you cannot always think you could have prevented it.

Son, things happen for a reason and that reason is My will, when you have faith and trust and you pray for good will, you will come to realize and know it was part of My plan". With faith, hope never dies…

I know God makes things happen, and he allows things to happen. I know I'm a part of Gods plan because I'm still here and so are you. Remember love is just a word until you put it between you and I, so if nobody has told you they love you today, I love you and God does too.

~COFFEE WITH GOD~

This morning I asked God about *"Coffee with God"*. He said, "Son, *"Coffee with God"* is how you start your day, you share our talks and inspirations with others. Those who know you know of Me. It has made your love for family, friends and brought happiness to your life. Our relationship is greater than it has ever been and you have found faith and trust in Me.

Sharing *CWG* with others has allowed others to find their way also". When I realized my life was changing for the better, I knew God had always been with me, I just didn't know how to talk to Him. I have faith, hope, and trust in Him because even when things didn't seem as though they were looking good they were actually getting better.

If you haven't found a way to talk to God, please do. Remember love is just a word until you put it between you and I, so if nobody has told you they love you today, I love you and God does too.

~COFFEE WITH GOD~

This morning I asked God about dancing with the stars. He said, "Son, when you have a circle of family and friends and they all seek positive influences and have a positive outlook on life, you're in the company of the right people. You wish the best for others and you actually know what you want out of life instead of wandering aimlessly with no direction.

Son, the reason why your life gets better each day is because you have direction, you make decisions which have good purpose and you love your life. Remember your old way of life and how it didn't matter who your friends or associates were and what they were about, that's when you were doing dances with wolves.

Now you have changed your direction, your thoughts, you are now accountable and responsible for your actions, now you are dancing with the stars!

Son, keep up the good work and continue to share your positive messages".

Remember love is just a word until you put it between you and I, so if nobody has told you they love you today, I love you and God does too.

~COFFEE WITH GOD~

This morning I asked God about deep water. He said, "Son, as you go forward in your life and leave the past behind you, there will be both obstacles and people who may become a negative influence.

Don't let the inner workings of others or society, stop you from your dreams or your goals. Keep your head up and your heart in it, and use the tools you have acquired from your new way of life and the positive people in your life.

Always make a plan for what your goals are and how you can achieve them, keeping track of your efforts, and learning from your mistakes. Anyone can have a dream, but not everyone will continue their journey because they think they see deep water ahead.

If you have faith, remember son, I always walk with you and the water is not as deep as you think". Remember love is just a word until you put it between you and I, so if nobody has told you they love you today, I love you and God does too.

~COFFEE WITH GOD~

This morning I asked God about class time. He said, "Son, anyone can go to school and put their books in a locker, but it's up to you to study so you can learn about life and look back on your lessons learned.

Each experience will come with a lesson and the learning experiences of life will always have a tool attached. It's up to you to hold on to the tools you get from your experiences and your mistakes. Everyone makes mistakes and they don't always have to have a bad outcome. Sometimes the solutions are in your mistakes, these will be called lessons learned.

Stay away from complacency, bad influences, and negative situations, and focus on the road ahead. Don't occupy your days with negative activities, these types of days only breed stagnate ideas, and there is nothing positive with no direction.

Son, life is like going to school, if you just go to class and not participate you lose interest. If you go to class and participate, as in life, you find that life is what you make of it". Remember love is just a word until you put it between you and I, so if nobody has told you they love you today, I love you and God does too.

~COFFEE WITH GOD~

This morning I asked God about learning from others. He said, "Son, you will meet a lot of people in your life and each one can teach one, no matter bad or good. Things can be learned from any and all, the unseen can be sought, the unspoken can be heard, the lost can be found, and the misguided can be forgiven. Life is a reality and the truth can be a learning experience". Remember love is just a word until you put it between you and I, so if nobody has told you they love you today, I love you and God does too.

~COFFEE WITH GOD~

This morning I asked God about the pink cloud. He said, "Son, your life is headed in the right direction, you have found a new way of life and you keep negative emotions under control.

The reality of life has now become an enriching, learning experience and you feel like you're walking on sunshine. Well son this euphoria you feel is known as the "pink cloud", but you must stay grounded and balanced in order for the blessings to become gifts.

Don't expect every day to seem like you have won the lottery, but treat each day as a lottery entry and the payoff is you may continue to ride that pink cloud. Staying positive, avoiding the negative, reaching and teaching, and never looking down on anyone unless you are helping them up, will keep you on the pink cloud.

If you get to a point where your ego becomes more important, or you think you are better than anyone, your cloud is no longer pink and the thunderstorm will soon follow.

Son, there is nothing wrong with feeling good about life and there's nothing wrong with riding the pink cloud, as long as you don't mind others riding with you". Remember love is just a word until you put it between you and I, so if nobody has told you they love you today, I love you and God does too.

~COFFEE WITH GOD~

This morning I asked God about perseverance. He said, "Son, first you must learn acceptance, everyone is different, some people don't care and others are not aware. It's not how your treated, it's how you react to others, situations, and unexpected obstacles in life.

Understand, not every person is able to face life on life's terms, sometimes there is a meltdown and the damage can be minimal or you can have tolerance and keep moving. No road is ever completely smooth, no snowflake is ever duplicated and no one is ever perfect, but it doesn't mean you can't make something of yourself just because of a few obstacles.

There may be bridges to cross a river, and many roads to get to any bridge. Some roads will take you in a direction which may or may not take you to where you want to go right away.

Son, with prayer and perseverance anything is possible, you can use any bridge to cross any river but never give up on a dream and don't burn that

bridge, you may need to cross it again someday".
Remember love is just a word until you put it
between you and I, so if nobody has told you they
love you today, I love you and God does too.

~COFFEE WITH GOD~

This morning I asked God about detox. He said, "Son, when the mind and body have become tainted, touched, or intoxicated with foreign substances or materials, it needs to be detoxed.

The mind has been convinced it needs certain things and it can become an obsession. While the process of a developing and obsessive appetite becomes an obstacle, the mind, body, and family will suffer as a result of the neglect. When you come to a point when you either realize or when you come to a place known as rock bottom, you need to detox, mind, body, and soul.

It's not just the physical and the mental, it's an obsession that needs to be addressed and treated. The recovery and renovation process can only begin with a detox, this includes ridding all mind and body of toxins, and this also may include toxic people.

Son, in your life you have many toxic obstacles, but if a person wants a better way of life they need to detox and cleanse". Remember love is just a word until you put it between you and I, so if nobody has told you they love you today, I love you and God does too.

~COFFEE WITH GOD~

This morning I asked God about insecurity. He said, "Son, if you have things going on in your life which make you feel uncomfortable, you may not be in the right place.

The places you may go in your life may conflict with who you are and what you want out of life. It may take your heart and soul to a place you don't need to be.

Son, it takes time to find your comfort zone in your mind, your heart, and in your soul. Until you find your comfort zone, you may feel insecure. The feeling of insecurity is something many people go through when they don't have confidence inside their heart and mind.

Understanding others is not an easy thing to do and the world can sometimes be a mean, cruel, and complicated place, but it all starts with learning to understand who you are first. Find security in knowing who you are, loving yourself, and being able to accept and respect others.

Son, not everyone will respect what you do and some wont respect who you are, but don't let the insecurities of others turn you into someone you are not. Believe in yourself, you are somebody, be your own person, and let no one dictate who you should be". Remember love is just a word until you put it between you and I, so if nobody has told you they love you today, I love you and God does too.

~COFFEE WITH GOD~

This morning I asked God about touching the world. He said, "Son, sometimes the finer things in life will let you know you have made a difference in someone's life. You don't need to keep score of all the good things you have done for people in your life, just know it won't go unrewarded.

Spending time with family and friends even if it's not a holiday is how you can touch lives. Every day you find out in one way or another life is short and no one will ever know when it is their time. Appreciate life and be grateful for the quality time you can spend with others, don't steal time from your loved ones by putting off family events.

Every morning when I wake you, it's My blessing to you and your gift is what you make of your day by being grateful for family and friends and those memorable times.

Son, there are some who may not get to experience the finer things in life because of their choices, like family, friends, love and respect, but if you pray for them you can help touch the world".

I hope you have a great day, and take the time and spend some quality time with family and friends. Remember love is just a word until you put it between you and I, so if nobody has told you they love you today, I love you and God does too.

~COFFEE WITH GOD~

This morning I asked God about one day at a time. He said, "Son, everyone has 24 hours in a day, no more, no less. With each day you embrace, you will have learned something more about life and its obstacles, these are the experiences which become the lessons of life.

Everyday many different things can and will happen, people will come and go and yet your life will still go on, with or without the drama. The important thing is you realize you have a tool box with tools to help you cope with obstacles that may appear out of nowhere. Don't be surprised, anything is possible, and you have a tool to help you get through it, and it's always best to start your day off with prayer.

There might be a time when you wake up from one of those bad dreams from your past and you ask, "Where did this come from"? Son, you live with the many events of your past running through your mind and they may pop up at any time, even while you sleep. Don't dwell on it, don't try to figure it out, don't let it keep you from your goals, just know your life is being renovated and it will get better one day at a time". Remember love is just a word until you put it between you and I, so if nobody has told you they love you today, I love you and God does too.

~COFFEE WITH GOD~

This morning I asked God about love. He said, "Son, some people won't get to experience love or even have people in their life that will care about them. Some people will misunderstand or make assumptions when you tell someone you love them.

Son, the important thing is you know I love you, and you want others to experience love in a caring and spiritual way. When you tell others you love them don't always expect them to say it back, and that's ok, many people don't know how to handle those three words. Those three words can mean so much to someone at any given time and it's also important that its known when you say it, it doesn't mean you're in love with them, but you care about them.

Son, don't ever stop sharing those three words, because you have touched so many with those words". You don't have to look for the people God puts in your life, just look for the life that God has put in you!

Remember love is just a word until you put it between you and I, so if nobody has told you they love you today, I love you and God does too.

~COFFEE WITH GOD~

This morning I asked God about cause and effect. He said, "Son, you have learned many things in life, about you, about your friends and about your family. You have a lot of things you have experienced and many lessons have been learned.

One thing you have come to realize in life is with every action there will be a reaction, whether it's a negative or a positive, the end results are the effect. Many things you may want out of life will sometimes be affected by your decisions and unfortunately it may have a negative effect on those you love. Think things through and pray before you say or do something that will impact the life of another.

The important thing is to try and not regret a decision once it has been made, it may become a resentment and you can't move on. Everything will happen one day at a time and every day you may be faced with a decision you have to make with concerns of your goals.

Prayer is your main tool and I will help you get through it, and not everyone will always understand you or your decisions, so focus on your goals and keep your head up and your heart in it.

Remember, you are focused on a vision and when you reach your goal you will feel the effect". Remember love is just a word until you put it between you and I, so if nobody has told you they love you today, I love you and God does too.

~COFFEE WITH GOD~

This morning I asked God about hidden treasures. He said, "Son, there are a lot of things in life that won't seem so obvious. There will be a lot of things in and around your life which appear to have no meaning or have no purpose. In time you will come to realize some things have a value, most everything has a meaning, but everyone has a purpose.

Even when things aren't apparent at the time, you may realize later on in life I have put something or someone in your life for a reason. Never discount an event in your life, everything happens for a reason and that reason is My will.

As you mature in life, as you add more tools to your tool box, as you find your life is becoming enriched in a way you never thought possible, things become more positive. The reality of it all is you have found hidden treasures in life and it's all because you have decided to turn your will and your life over to Me".

My life is full of hidden treasures and the joys in my life have become so apparent I don't ever want to go back to my old way of life. Remember love is just a word until you put it between you and I, so if nobody has told you they love you today, I love you and God does too.

~COFFEE WITH GOD~

This morning I asked God about good intentions. He said, "Son, many times you tried to reach out and help someone with kind and supportive words, a hug, a caring smile, or even giving a stranger food or money so they can eat.

There is always going to be someone in need of something and sometimes you are there to help. Your heart is compassionate and you have understanding because in your past you have been down, you have the disease of addiction, you have relapsed, you have hit rock bottom and you know what it's like to be homeless.

The important thing is to know you can't always help everyone by yourself, but you know how to extend a resource for those you can help. Sometimes it's not what you know, it's who you know, and many resources are available to the people you meet who are in need.

Son, you, like many have went through some tough times in your life, you have found a way to turn your life around because someone showed you how to love yourself. Finding out what it really means to be grateful, because you do care about others.

Son, you can't always help everyone, but it starts with prayer and those are good intentions". Remember love is just a word until you put it between you and I, so if nobody has told you they love you today, I love you and God does too.

~COFFEE WITH GOD~

This morning I asked God about foundation. He said, "Son, every event which has happened in your life may come to memory every once in a while, and it may come at a time when you need it the most. This could come from the memory of lessons learned, or you can find this tool in your tool box and it will be marked "solution". No matter what the outcome, this will become something in your life that may help you in your future.

Anyone can meet someone who may or may not leave a positive thought, regardless it will become a memory. These events, these memories, and the results, will become part of your foundation for your life. The reason being is anything in your life you experience, can determine how you could react to a similar situation. If you always tend to react in a negative way, the structure in your life will have a defect in the foundations that you may build your morals and your character on.

Son, anything built with a defective foundation can weaken and eventually fall or inevitably hit rock bottom. A good foundation starts with good morals and good character. Son, your foundation is only as strong as your faith".

Remember love is just a word until you put it between you and I, so if nobody has told you they love you today, I love you and God does too.

~COFFEE WITH GOD~

This morning I asked God about life changers. He said, "Son, you may never know when you might read something, see someone, or hear words of wisdom from the least expected, don't take it for granted.

You have many resources around you that can always help you to improve your life, not just mentally but physically as well. Renovation doesn't just mean changing the interior, it means changing your foundation, and the exterior as well.

The cold stare which use to occupy your face has now turned into a smile you share with others. Knowing your dreams are now possible you are able to share with others that, "Ain't no mountain high enough", and with prayer anything is possible.

Son, the people you have in your life believe in you and you believe in yourself. You may become somebody's life changer, and they may become life changers also.

It's all about being positive son, and it's what you make of life which makes you the better person you have become today. Everything you experience in life can be a part of your tool box, but anyone you experience in life can be a life changer". Remember love is just a word until you put it between you and I, so if nobody has told you they love you today, I love you and God does too.

~COFFEE WITH GOD~

This morning I asked God about long term investments. He said, "Son, each day I wake you, make an investment in your day by praying and asking for courage, guidance, and strength.

You have come to realize your life is a blessing and the gift is being grateful for what you have in life. It's not the material things in life that have the meaning, it's the spiritual soul you have developed inside, it's the core of your courage and strength.

The tools you have gathered in your new way of life, the ones you use on a daily basis, the ones you share with others, are what has enriched your life. Son, I say this to you often and it's very important you remember this, never look down on someone unless you're helping them up.

There will be many obstacles in your life, good and bad, and it's not how you're treated, it's how you react to your situation which makes you a better person. Learning from your mistakes and always seeking to improve your life is a long term investment". Remember love is just a word until you put it between you and I, so if nobody has told you they love you today, I love you and God does too.

~COFFEE WITH GOD~

This morning I want to share with you one of the many unique ways God has blessed my life. All my life I only remember one person who I have called Mom, I call her Mom, and she is my Mother.

Many will call someone significant as this person many different terms of endearment. The title of mother is given, and there are some expectations which come with the name, but it is also earned and sometimes in a very tough way.

Ever since I can think back, my Mom has always been there for me, and she has never let me down and has loved me unconditionally. One of the reasons I am who I am is because my Mother raised me to be who God wants me to be.

Despite my addiction, all the good, the bad, and the ugly in my life, my Mom still continues to call me her son. I am so very grateful my Mother still exists in my life, and we always say "I love you". I wish everyone could have a Mom like mine. Maybe the world would be a better place. I know many people can't ever have the experience of love I have with my family, but break the cycle and share this type of love with others and you will find happiness in your heart.

Remember love is just a word until you put it between you and I, so if nobody has told you they love you today, I love you and God does too.

Happy Mother's Day to all the Mothers out there and to all the Fathers who have to be a Mother too!

Happy Mother's Day Mom…I love you so very much.

~COFFEE WITH GOD~

This morning I want to say Happy Fathers Day to all the fathers and share with you how God blessed my life~~~

Dad, thank you so much for being a part of my life, not just as a Father, but a proud Father. No matter what I have done throughout my life, you have always and still continue to call me your son. I have taken my mistakes and learned from them and I have been able to say thank you Dad for all the mistakes I have made and how you still continue to teach me.

You have instilled many great traits in me which have been recognized by others. So much so, I have been commended on the great job you have done, and I continue to carry your morals in my life, good manners, compassion for others and the true meaning of family.

Dad, the definition of "Dad" in my dictionary only has a picture, only because God hasn't created a word to describe how much I appreciate you in my life, and that's because my life as a man started from your teachings, your presence in my life and the love you have always given us. Dad, I respect you as a man, as a provider, as a friend, as a brother, a husband, an uncle, a grandfather, a co-worker, a neighbor, and the greatest Father a son could ever have.

If anyone who reads this isn't being a father to their child or children, stop and start being their dad. No child deserves to not have at least a father figure in their life. Remember love is just a word until you put it between you and I, so if nobody has told you they love you today, I love you and God does too.

Happy Fathers Day Dad I love you very much!

~COFFEE WITH GOD~

This morning I asked God about finding faults in others. He said, "Son, why do feel you need to find faults in others? This would be an indication you are allowing your ego to take the place of your morals. It would also mean you are judging others and this would not be one of the tools in your tool box.

People make mistakes every day and sometimes those mistakes may involve you, directly or indirectly, accusations or suspicions from others may become resentments. Son, it's unfortunate when others try to find fault in you, even when you know you're not wrong. Praying for serenity is a good start, courage is what it takes to accept you cannot always change the thoughts of others, but you can pray for the wisdom to know the difference.

It takes time for some to realize they may have been wrong, and maybe they will never admit to making a mistake. Still it's never a good idea to try and find the faults in others, remember son, at one time you were there also".

Remember love is just a word until you put it between you and I, so if nobody has told you they love you today, I love you and God does too.

~COFFEE WITH GOD~

This morning I asked God why he does things for me? He said, "Son, you have had quite a journey to become the person you are today, and you have had many experiences. The lessons you have learned, have become the tools that now exist in your tool box. Those tools are used in your everyday life and you have shared them with others who now find comfort in knowing life doesn't always have to be an uphill climb.

I don't give you things because you deserve them, don't think I give you things because you have earned them, son, I bless you with things because, I love you".

I have dreams and goals in my life now and I don't have expectations of what God does for me, I trust and have faith he loves me and he is with me always, as he is with you. Remember, love is just a word until you put it between you and I, so if nobody has told you they love you today, I love you and God does too.

~~~TO WHOM IT MAY CONCERN~~~

It's not FOR me to judge what you think of me...thank you for being a part of my life and my recovery.

It's so unfortunate people go through life and always continue to think someone else is to blame for the road in their journey of life...meanwhile resentments or regrets manifest...for me, no regrets, no resentments.

I don't forget the things people have done for me and I don't keep tabs on what I have done for others.

All I know is this, God has and never will make mistakes, and it wasn't by mistake our lives enmeshed.

People make decisions every day to sever ties, that's life, my decision is to always keep people in my heart and in my prayers.

I'm not perfect and I do make mistakes, so "to whom it may concern"...thank you for being a part of my recovery and my life.

~COFFEE WITH GOD~

This morning I asked God about progress. He said, "Son, every day you move closer to something in your life, whether it's bad, good, expected or unexpected. Your life has greatly changed in a positive way, you have made progress and you continue to do positive things in your life and in the lives of others.

Progress is a constant motion, and it may become a slow process, but you must never give up. Progress can be a daily achievement, a goal in life, an amends or just simply taking one day at a time.

Son, everyone in life will have ups and downs, and some will feel defeat at the first obstacle. Obstacles may become an immeasurable way to progress at a point in your life where you never thought anything was possible.

Progress comes with perseverance, progress comes with patience, acceptance helps in progress and most of all prayer is always a way to help achieve progress.

Son, progress only stops when you give up, so keep your head up and your heart in it, and never give up".

It took me awhile, and it took progress, not perfection, to become the person I am today…never give up on progress!!! One day at a time. Remember love is just a word until you put it between you and I, so if nobody has told you they love you today, I love you and God does too.

~COFFEE WITH GOD~

This morning I would like to thank God for blessing me with the greatest Father next to God…my Dads birthday is today and I'm so proud to have him as my Dad. Dad thank you so very much for all you have done to instill in me the greatest of morals, values of life, respect of myself, and of others. The honesty you have taught me and the understanding and acceptance of the facts of life, have helped me to become the person I am today.

Dad, you have no idea how grateful, and how much I appreciate all you and Mom have done, not just for me, but for this family and all the people you have touched. Dad, it truly is a blessing to have you in my life and I wouldn't trade it for the world. It seems we have become traveling buddies since I decided to turn my life around back in June 2007, and the true experience of a Father-son relationship is very enriching, and I am so grateful God has allowed us this chance in our life.

Happy Birthday Dad!

I love you very much and thank you for being the ultimate Dad, in my heart and in my life.

Remember love is just a word until you put it between you and I, so if nobody has told you they love you today, I love you and God does too.

~COFFEE WITH GOD~

This morning I would like to share something with you. Only God can make things happen and allow things to happen in a person's life. There are no accidents, no coincidences, we all have a purpose, a reason, a meaning in life and only God knows...it is his will.

We find out things every day about ourselves and what we are capable of doing. We all have the ability to become a "life changer". The awesome beauty of this is we never know whose life we may change. We may never ever find out, but know this, someone is always watching you and listening to you, not just God, but someone who needs to hear or see you and the way your life has changed for the better.

All you have done in your past, the good, the bad and the ugly has allowed us to be a part of each other's lives, and together I believe we can help make the world a better place.

Remember love is just a word until you put it between you and I, so if nobody has told you they love you today, I love you and God does too.

~INSPIRATION~

This morning I asked God about being a creature of habit. He said, "Son, you have the ability to learn things every day, some old, some new. It's up to you to decide what things you will keep in your tool box and maintain in your life as a learning tool.

Certain things will become habits, and now you have become a creature of habit, doing things on a regular basis. It starts off being a weekend warrior and then you find out that Monday never comes. Being a creature of habit can be a good thing but don't let the habit become a creature in you.

~COFFEE WITH GOD~

This morning I asked God about visions. He said, "Son, when your life was clouded with poor judgments and bad decisions, you had no vision. Now you have decided to renovate your life, you have begun to make long term investments. This is because you see life as a reality and know your foundation is only as strong as your faith. You know what you want in life and it has everything to do with a better way of life. Doing the right thing so the right things will happen, and having love in your heart and praying for others. Remember love is just a word until you put it between you and I, so if nobody has told you they love you today, I love you and God does too.

~COFFEE WITH GOD~

CHRISTMAS

This morning…please take a moment…first, I would like to wish everyone a very Merry Christmas, may God bless you and your family/friends. Please take a moment to know there are others who won't get to experience Christmas, for many different reasons, some will be away from their family because they are serving our country.

Some will be homeless and barely have shelter to protect them from the weather. Some will be incarcerated, or in an institution of some sort. Please take a moment to realize some people will feel slighted because they didn't get the gift they wanted or the one they were expecting. Please take a moment to understand Christmas is about giving. Please take a moment to know there are children who won't get a gift this year, for many different reasons.

Please take a moment to know you are blessed in one way or another, and someone may wish they had what you have. If you are reading this, you are blessed, you have eyes, some may not…you can read…some cannot.

Don't wait until this one day a year to give, find it in your heart to give more than just this one day a year. It doesn't have to be anything material, give a smile, give a hug, and give your time to someone who may not have anyone in their life. Remember, handshakes are for business deals, hugs are for saving lives. Never miss that chance to say "I love you".

Remember love is just a word until you put it between you and I, so if nobody has told you they love you today, I love you and God does too.

Merry Christmas everyone and may God bless your life in a way like he has blessed mine.

Character defects; things I'm doing that I shouldn't be doing. Shortcomings; things I'm not doing that I should be doing....

~INSPIRATION~

This morning when God woke me I immediately thanked Him, then I opened my laptop to share this...

Last year I was blessed with new people, places, and things, much of it in a very positive way. Not all last year was filled with positive events, but throughout the negative events; I still choose not to put mind altering substances in my body. I'm so grateful that I have renovated my life, and God has everything to do with it.

When God allows you to experience things in life, and you persevere it's so you may one day share your experience, strength and hope and become a life changer.

God thank you for putting certain people in my life, as they move on, I guess I should do the same.

Hello family, my name is Randy Ran and I am an addict…my clean date is June 2007. I didn't find God in church, I found him in recovery. In doing so he uses me as a messenger, and it took 30 years of my disease to get me to where I am now.

I post *Coffee with God* every morning and I have done so every morning since February 2011. At one time, I was posting it in over 30 Facebook groups every morning. In December 2011 one of my Facebook friends suggested I create a page on Facebook. Since then it has been read by almost two million people around the world, translated into over 18 languages and in over 25 countries.

I give you that information because recovery/renovation isn't about me, it's about us. There is so much negativity on Facebook I wanted to make a difference. I wanted to be a part of the "balance". I don't hear Gods voice in my head, I hear his voice in my heart. I don't have the capability to make my morning messages up. I know God has put a spirit in me that allows me to express feelings, and have a better understanding of the way my life should be from now on.

We all have our ups and downs, we all face life in our own way and we all have others in our lives that may not have the best suggestions but they mean well. I find this out in more ways than one, especially when I write, it allows me the time to reflect, and hear what God is telling me.

I know that in recovery it requires renovation, just like when you renovate a house, you start with the foundation.

INSPIRATIONS

- GOD said "…there were people in your past who took you where they wanted you to be, today there are people who will tell you where you should be, follow Me son and I will take you where you need to be"

- The only time you look down at someone is when you're helping them up

- You can't change time, but you can change things in time, progress takes time and change is a part of that

- It is possible many won't realize how wonderful life is, while they can't appreciate up, until they have been down

- If your heart isn't in it, there is no hope, if you don't believe in yourself, there is no faith

- Choose a road which will allow you to reach your goals and not a road where there are many obstacles marked, "I gave up here"

- You see far because you stand on the shoulders of giants

- It's not how your treated, it's how you react to it which will make you a better person

- If we walk together we can talk together, if we meet together we can eat together and when we pray together we can stay together

- Resentments create hostages

- Some days will be better than others, but no days have to be like they were before

- Obligation does not make a relationship, and a relationship will not complete who you are

- GOD said "… don't hit the snooze button on your life, you never know what I have planned for you"

- GOD said "…anything I give you is a blessing, what you choose to do with it becomes the gift"

- God doesn't give me things because I deserve them. God doesn't give me things because I think I have earned them, He blesses me with things because He loves me

- Your foundation is only as strong as your faith and with faith, hope never dies

- Many have tried to do it alone and find the only thing they are good at doing alone is digging a deeper hole

- It's unfortunate some people start off trying to be a weekend warrior and eventually they find that Monday never comes

- Real friends walk in when the rest of the world walks out

- Don't look behind you to see who has your back, look beside you and find out who walks with you

- Prayer doesn't have to be a ritual thing, let it be a natural thing

- Resentments are like anchors, they will slow you down and even stop you from moving on in life

- Success is not of material things, but of the values in your life

- T.G.I.F. =TRUSTING GOD IS FAITH

- Don't be surprised at what others will do, be amazed at all the good you can do

- Your past is now the wisdom of your future

- God will always reveal to those in the dark, what self has discovered with His light

- T.G.I.F. =TODAYS GIFT IS FREEDOM

- Handshakes are for business deals, hugs are for saving lives

- Some people have come and gone in my life, I thank God you are not one of them

- The obstacles you thought were mountains were only speed bumps

- T.G.I.F.=TODAYS GIFT IS FAMILY

- Don't let the insecurities of others turn you into someone you are not

- You don't have to look for the people God puts in your life, just look for the life that God has put in you

- Progress only stops when you give up

- When God allows you to experience things in life, and you persevere it's so you may one day share your experience, strength and hope and become a life changer

- I'm not proud of the mistakes that I've made, but I'm proud that I can admit that I made them

- When you talk to God, you have His undivided attention

- T.G.I.F.=THANKING GOD IS FIRST

I TRULY BELIEVE THIS…

IF WE MEET TOGETHER

WE CAN EAT TOGETHER

IF WE WALK TOGETHER

WE CAN TALK TOGETHER

AND…

IF WE PRAY TOGETHER

WE CAN STAY TOGETHER.

People that inspire me

My whole entire Family inspires me, supports me and has loved me unconditionally.

Oprah, Joel Osteen, Tyler Perry, Dr. Drew, Damon James (aka Dj Pizo), Jason George, Samuel L. Jackson, Robert Downey Jr. Tom Sizemore, Ice Cube, George Clinton,

COFFEE WITH GOD by

RANDY RAN

THE EXPANDED EDITION

~~~THANK YOU~~~

First I want to thank God, without Him I am nothing. My parents Dina and Lou, thank you for being the greatest parents any children could ever dream of having in their lives. Despite all my mistakes, you have loved me unconditionally and still call me your son.

My oldest sister, even though we don't nearly talk as much as we used to, I will always love you.

Dana, my brother, you may be younger than me, but I will always look up to you. Thank you so much for being one of my heroes.

Kenya, I love you so much, you have always been in my corner, supported me and lifted me up when I was down. You truly are the Worlds Greatest Sister!!!

Terry "Ta Ta" Wilkerson, Frank "Mister" Wilkerson and Donald Seay thank you so much for all the laughs, and the heart to heart support. The Wilkerson family, John Adams, Barbara Davis-Gibson, the Adams family, the Davis family, the Holt family, the Saffords and the Wallaces.

Ms Connie Thomas, Frank, Larlee, Maggie, Andrew (Flitty), Conrad, Mark, Chris, Madalene (RIP), Paul, Cathy, Angie, Nicole, and Michelle…The Thomas family, and all the nieces and nephews.

Brian "Brotha B" Carter I love you man, I promise you Madalene will never ever be forgotten.

Chuck Richard, and the rest of my family in Lincoln Village, Sacramento Ca.

Kathy Hopkins thank you so much for still being my friend, despite all that I put you through we can still be friends.

My sons Christopher (Chris) and Michael (Mr Mike) Bocanegra, Im so proud of the both of you.

Andrea, I will never forget what you told me at your wedding…"Thank you for being the father I never had"

My grandkids, Adrian and Chelsea, I love you both so much.

My nephew and nieces, Orlando, and Tionna Wilkerson, Remington, Jayla and Jazzi George.

My extended family since I was born, the Walkers, Uncle James, Aunt Carol, Shari, Shelley and Jay.

The Shaw brothers Greg and Tracy, thank you so much for the memories and still being a part of my life.

Bob, Becky and Gabe George, thank you for your love, support and being a part of our families.

St Gerard Falcons Class of 76, Marie Lewis thank you so much.

Mark Digirolamo, (Quarterback of the St Gerard Falcons), I am so grateful God put you back in my life, even if you never threw me a pass or gave me a handoff, you always lead us to a win.

Hiram W. Johnson Warriors class of 80

My four Warriors who have been with CWG since day 1...Terri Susan Walsh, Alison Penrose DeKreek, Lynette Lenzi and John Orta thank you so much.

Georgia Burris-Jaye, thank you so much for always being there for me, I love you JoJo.

Diana and Bill Gutierrez thank you for your prayers and support.

The Carranzas, Crespos, and the Wahls

Dale Eszlinger aka Mr. Earnhardt I love you brother

Michael Wilson, my Brother, I love you so much. Ebony you have made an impact in our lives thank you so much for being a part of our family.

Wil Dub Studio and my Nephews, Zaron aka Z-Block, Clay aka ClayzeeJay, Cory Lacy aka MGM Cory and Lawrence Clark aka LoLo. I know with God and you keep your heads up and your hearts in it, nothing is impossible. I love you Nephews.

Shanna Wilson you are such a strong person and my lil sister, I love you and thank you so much.

The Brantleys, Jim (RIP), Barbara, Robert and Peter. Growing up I never thought it was possible to have contact with old neighbors after 40 years. I am so grateful that we are still in each others lives.

Wayne Stapleton, I am so proud of you, lol, I always knew you were going to be a "Sports Wikipedia".

Blackstone and Zoom…There are only a few who will know how much this means to me, and us. My childhood was so blessed with friends, that I now call Family. One day we must all get together and visit our old "stomping grounds".

To all my Facebook friends, that I now call my Family, thank you all so very much for the love and support you have given me. My CWG family that have lifted my spirits and have inspired more than just me, a special thank you.

Sharon Osborne

Donald Bayer aka DJ

Donna Wall

Sandee Riffel

Karen Simmons

Lisa KeepingItonehundra Quash

De'Bora Brown-Brooks

Sandy Beers

Rod Ferrer

Nancy Carolla-Lazarian

Rhonda Reid

Tina McKoy Hall

Kelly Kettle

Deana L Binion

Dinky Gaskins Bender

Duane Cox-thank you so much for the banner picture on my CWG page

Donna Zurfluh

Joehuny-thank u 4 lifting me up

Maureen Richardson-thank you so much for my work boots

Cindy Agostini

Justin Hintz-thank you so much for the opportunity to work with you again, and these, my co-workers and new friends.

I started working at my current job in December 2011, since then I have met many people from all walks of life. When you have a job description that allows you to interact with many people each day, it can make your work day something to look forward to all the time. These are some of the people that I have fun working with almost every day.

Scottie Carlson-thank you for being a part of my recovery from the beginning.

Gary Mejia-you and I have become best friends and I really appreciate you.

Laura Taylor-I can not thank you enough for all your help with my book

Kenny Bishop

Jim McQuade

Reed Barnes

Duane Duvall

Marvin Towles

JC Kaestner

Jon Cobb

Daniel Lopez

Matthew
Marburg

Wendy Brown

Chris "Bangs"

Sean Foster

Ivan K

Darin
Encallado

Josh
Altamirano

Jason Ramirez

Travis Tully

Jesus Aromin

Ryan Gardner

Andrew
Doughty

Nate Potter

Petr Artyushevskiy Sr

Peter Artyushevskiy Jr

Stephanie
Shaltes

Chris Glau

Nikolay Oliferchik

Beth Stireman

These are the last pages in this book, and these people have a part in helping me put all the previous pages together.

My Sincerest and Deepest Thanks to Each One of You.

Gail Jacobs Johnson, you have helped me more than you will ever know. I can honestly say this, if not for you these 2 books do not exist, I love you Gail.

Sarah "Pinky" Welch, you truly are an inspiration to the world, your contributions go unseen and that takes a special person to continue even when not many know how you save lives.

Jim Bowers, your artwork on the front cover of my first book set things in motion my friend, thank you so much for your contribution.

Author Michael Charles Givens, you guided me just when I was getting ready to give up, thank you so much for showing up when I didn't even ask.

Taiwo Ayodele Ajayi, your suggestions and your guidance help set things in motion, thank you so much Taiwo.

Alison Diprose Murphy, thank you, your idea to create the page "Coffee with God by Randy Ran", put me on the right path.

Dj Pizo, aka Damon James, thank you so much for being such an inspiration, I love talking to you man you have so much knowledge, please share it.

Nancy Maritza Trujillo, I love you and you have become such an inspiration and a beautiful Butterfly, not just for me, but for so many others. I thank God for you every day, and you have helped me to find myself and allowed me to share my life with you, Ashley (Ash) & Alexis(Ellie).

Duane Cox, I know God has put people in my life at different times, and for different reasons. I am so grateful that you put magic in my life by your creative artwork, thank you so very much for my book cover.

WHEN YOU TALK

TO GOD YOU WILL

HAVE HIS

UNDIVIDED

ATTENTION